BEING ME

GRADY NUTT

BEING ME

BROADMAN PRESS
NASHVILLE, TENNESSEE

Library of Congress Catalog Card Number: 71–145984
Dewey Decimal Classification: 248.8
Printed in the United States of America

DEDICATION

To my father, Grady C. Nutt,
       whom I almost always misunderstood
       whose love and approval I've thirsted for
       who walked the second mile for me
       whose love and approval I have
       who makes me stand tall when I hear the word
           Father.
Thanks, Dad.

CONTENTS

SELF, YOU BUG ME!

You change constantly

> follow distant stars
>> love
>>> hate
>>>> feel assurance
>>>>> know despair.

There's a plateau I'm sure

> where life levels off
> and I won't be
> confused
>> bewildered
>>> uncertain or   lonely.

Isn't there?

Life keeps telling me *no*

> with the volume
> all the way up.

Now I'm the rope in a constant tug-of-war

> between who I think I am
> and who I'd like to be.

I have a cousin 21 years old

> a senior in college
> and he still doesn't know
> what he wants to do in life.

You'd think someone that far along

> would be confident
> ready to move out and take hold of life
> to help his world
> to start making helpful changes.   He's not.

So, Self, let's be honest

> with life
>> friends
>>> parents
>>>> and God.

Let's be me.

CHAPTER 1

I AM! I AM? I AM...

Words.

Like pollution, they surround and suffocate us.

Fish drown in what is supposedly good water
     people get lung cancer breathing city air
      geese die in oil slicks
        only enough tigers left in the world to
        make ten more coats
          while you choke
on words.

Well, here comes another bookful.

Special note: All these words are meant to be helpful
        meant to be friend and not foe
        meant to communicate and not condemn

meant to share understanding, not just dole
out simple solutions (that never
work, anyhow)
meant to trim your wick, not snuff your flame.

This sentence is our "clothesline"; we'll hang our book on it:

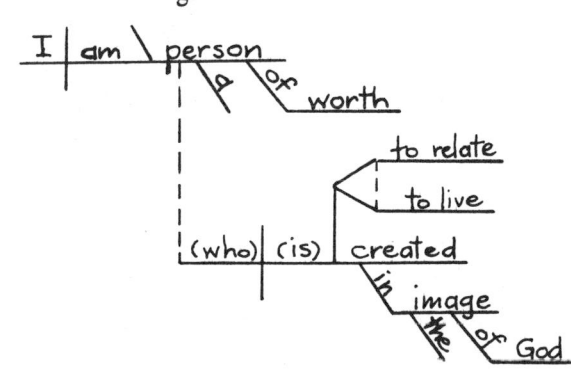

> "I am
> a person
> of worth
> created in the image of God
> to relate
> and to live!"

I am going to ask for ninety pages of your time
to diagram that sentence

to march around it like a maypole
to dissect it
to help you understand it.

Are you game? I really hope so.

Now, take this chapter for instance.
Can you imagine taking roughly one sixth of the book on just
two words?

To be honest, when I decided to do it I even thought that
myself. The more I thought about it though, the more the
idea began to crack its egg, and gradually
the gawky bird of an outline emerged,
wet-feathered,
and gained strength in my mind.

Here's the idea.

Each of us says "I am"
in different ways:
some with confidence
some with doubt
some with reservation.

That's the logic behind the three kinds of punctuation:

> "I am!"
> "I am?"
> "I am . . ."

Sound confusing? I hope not. The intention is to talk about a very common struggle of young people:

> becoming aware of yourself
> probing yourself
> risking yourself.

Each of these *I am*'s merits some "walking-through-barefooted." Slip off your boots and come along . . .

I AM!

Cassius Clay said it:

> "I am the greatest!"
> And we snickered
> 'til he beat Liston.

Paul Anderson could say it:

> "I am
> the strongest man in the world."
> He's proven it in every corner
> of the globe
> by lifting more weight than any human.

Neil Armstrong can say it:

> "I am
> the first human
> to set foot on another piece
> of celestial real estate."

Paul, apostle of note, said it:

> "I am
> the chief of sinners."
> (I run him a close second!)

God said it to Moses:

"I am!"

Jesus said it often:

"I am
the way
the truth
the life
the door
the bread of life
the water of life
the vine
the good shepherd."

Like Moses, barefoot on a rocky slope, before a burning bush,

ponder the great *I am,*
the *I am* that is
you.

There is an exclamation on this *I am* to show

self-awareness
self-assurance
self-affirmation.

Ever have a day when you loathed you, couldn't stand to see your reflection in the mirror, didn't understand yourself? Several reasons . . .

Early childhood is the time for other-control of your life.

> Parents.
> Teachers.
> Etc.

You rarely had to struggle to make decisions about your actions. Someone else spent full time doing it for you.

September 1 rolled around more often than Christmas

> and you had to go to school
> had to dress up for it
> had to watch your suntan fade
> had to eat the lunchroom food
> (sorry about that one!)
> had to do new math.

$$6 = 10_{(6)}$$
$$7 = 11_{(6)}$$
$$8 = 12_{(6)}$$
$$\overline{21_{(10)} = 33_{(6)}}$$

Church presented little problem for you then

> thanks to easy stuff like
> Noah
> David
> Moses

Paul's missionary journeys
Adam and Eve.

Church is seldom trouble when you learn about someone else.

Your parents held nightly conferences after your bedtime

> to plan your life tomorrow
> to plan your haircut
> to get the wrong kind of tennis shoes
> because *Consummer Report* said
> "These wear best!"

Then came freedom—not like a cannon shot, but like a
> mustard seed,
> slowly.

More and more you came to decide for yourself who you'd be

> and you caught the ball in the open
> and ran like mad.

No more total domination! (Hurrah!)
No more *Consumer Report* fashions! (Glory in the highest!)

Marilyn Maye says it in a secular hymn to individuality:

> "Make your own kind of music
> Sing your own kind of song
> Even if nobody else sings along . . ."

You are now a full-fledged, card-carrying, dues-paying

> *I am!*

Congratulations.

I believe that's your problem with the person you see in the mirror.

> *He* is now the one deciding for you.
> Not parents
> Not teachers
> Not etc.

Freedom to decide is primarily freedom to make good decisions,

> also.

So you stand there shaving or combing your hair

with *why* hanging heavy over your head . . .
and that brings us to the question mark on your

I am.

I AM?

Probing self is crucial to life, and the young years

are the zoo
where all your emotions
are on exhibit
to self and others.

It seems to me that a major shift has taken place in the last
few years.

We used to ask, "What am I going to do?"
You ask, "Who am I going to be?"

Allow me a paragraph for a change. Today's young people are
more concerned with *identity* than *function*. Knowing what

makes you tick and experiencing life honestly and completely makes a great deal more sense than playing the game of earning money, driving the latest car, having the right degrees, and other similar trappings. I have to take my hat off to you for that. But we have a serious problem: your parents and leaders have an almost impossible task in helping you because they never asked the same kinds of questions at the same age and they have little personal experience to go on in order to really understand how you feel. Hence, they give directions, react to your styles, and generally try to get you "down to serious business." Try a little tenderness with them, too, OK?

You now find yourself in the seed-planting time of life

> placing in the soil of what you *are*
> the promise of what you *can be*.

This makes your efforts at honesty with yourself and those around you quite crucial.

Here is a beautiful idea from Paul Tournier, Swiss psychiatrist and Christian gentleman:

> "What then is the frontier between what I am and what I can become? Who knows whether tomorrow my reactions to some new event will not reveal an aspect of my person more im-

portant than any I have so far discovered?
Is not what I shall be capable of tomorrow
contained in what I am today?" [1]

That really hits me where it helps! It means basically:

> know yourself well
> question yourself consistently
> aim for the highest that you can be
> struggle, but with hope.

You will very likely find the answer to the question "Who am
I?" to be very exciting:

> something like,
> "A great human being—
> worth knowing
> worth being
> worth loving."

That kind of answer makes a question worthwhile!

Which brings us to *I am* again.

> It has worn an exclamation point;
> it has worn a question mark;
> it now needs three parallel periods.

I AM . . .

A while back I mentioned three key components to self-understanding:

> becoming aware of yourself
> probing yourself
> risking yourself.

Welcome to risk!

The basic task ahead of you for life is this:

> to take the *I am* that you are
> put it against life as it is
> exert your uniqueness
> relate honestly to God and man
> and make the world more nearly
> what it ought to be because
> *you* passed this way.

Therefore, the three consecutive periods on this *I am*. They reflect

> uncertainty
> grappling
> testing your weight on thin ice
> preparation for full commitment.

To me, this is what *Being Me* is all about.

> "I am!"
> "I am?"
> "I am . . ."

And so you are . , ,

NOTES
1. Paul Tournier, *The Meaning of Persons* (New York: Harper and Row, 1957), pp. 13–14.

WHO WAS THAT MASKED STRANGER?

Every day is Halloween
     and I hide
     behind a mask
     and hold out my Kroger sack
     (biggest size)
     hoping to collect approval
     for my neat disguise.

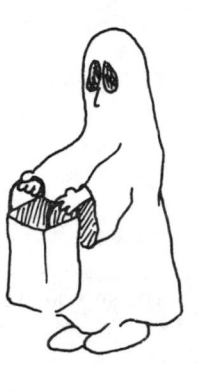

Nobody goes to a door of promise
     to knock for goodies
     wearing
     his real face.

Who'd give goodies to *that*?

Very *good* reasoning if you're seven
     playing
     pirate
       spook
         monster or
           witch.

Typical reasoning for an adolescent
     fearful
     that the real *me*
     will earn
     no goodies.

What would my sack contain
     if they saw
     what I see
     behind my mask?

A rejection?
     A scoff?
       A laugh?
         A put-down?

Could there possibly be
     acceptance
     love
     affirmation . . .
     like I *really* am?

CHAPTER 2

A PERSON

All that *mask* business

    has a very definite purpose.

We wear masks in our relationships

    mainly for
    two reasons:

        (1) to hide something
               from others
        (2) to play some role
               laid on us by
               family
                   friends
                      society
                        etc.

Ever do something a bit strange or unordinary

> and have the argument
> used on you:
> > "What would
> > people say?"

Right there your mask is being fitted

> over the
> real you.

Read this first part over again

> to be certain
> that I have *not* said:
> > "Family
> > society
> > and
> > friendly influences
> > > should not
> > > be heeded."

Nothing like that at all; rather,

> real maturity comes to you
> when you learn to read
> the difference
> between
> guidance (good influence)
> and
> pressure (bad influence).

This is the logical place to introduce

> two
> key words:
>> *personage*
>>> and
>>>> *person*

How about the simplest definitions

> before expanding
> each concept?

Personage will be used to define

> roles we play
> for approval
>> survival
>>> acceptance
>>> secrecy
>>>> assurance.

Person will carry the meaning of

> the self
> becoming aware of uniqueness
> through the living give
>>>> and
>>>> take
> of
>> playing roles
>> taking risks

          making mistakes
           knowing hurt
            finding encouragement
           hoping hope.

Let's unravel these two words

       like two
       old sweaters—
            stitch by stitch.

Personage.

Let me introduce my good friend,

       Dan Webster.

He points out an interesting fact:

       personage
       comes from the root word
       for *person*
       meaning "actor's mask."

I could quote you a bucket of footnotes

       to support my point
       that playing roles
       is normal
       and very important
       in the developing young person.

But you probably share my distaste

> for footnotes,
>> *ibid.*
>>> *op. cit.*
>>> and all.

Suffice it to say that most experts agree

> that the self
> is always in process—
>> in other words,
>> *becoming.*

Life constantly throws new challenges

> at you
> which you must
> absorb
> into your system
> of values.

It all starts with birth

> and the earliest realizations
> that you
> are not

a chair
   a fuzzy duck
      a bouncing ball
         or teddy bear.

Your parents came because you cried

      and sometimes
      cried
      because you came!

Between these truths—

      their pleasure when you joyed them
      their displeasure when you unjoyed them—
         you developed
         the fine art
         of mask-wearing.

Society also asked for its turn at bat

      in school
        in church
          on the playground
            in the neighborhood gang.

To be accepted by people around you

      you had to learn
      to live up to their expectations
         to play by their rules
            to avoid the things that irked them.

The non-chair, -duck, -ball, -bear

      that was the real *ye*
      quickly learned
      how to win friends
      and influence people.

And therein lies the reason for Webster's definition:

      the real you
      is always struggling
      for the proper way or ways
      in which
      to let the real you
      shine through.

Like a woman at a bargain hat counter

      you try one approach
         test another stance
         open a new branch office
         hide unpleasantness
         amplify accomplishment
         in the great hope

> that
> one
> will
> fit!

Personage, in summary, then is

> the decoration and icing
> on the cake of *person.*

The comedian Rodney Dangerfield has a great line:

> "My mother was so mean to me
> that on Halloween
> she made me go out
> without a mask!"

How cruel!

The mask of personage is like a cocoon

> that protects and nourishes
> the emerging person
> until he is ready
> to face life's midnight
> when we are unmasked
> and forced to face the music
> like we really are.

Person is best understood against that backdrop—

> the experience of testing one's self
> against life's forces
> in an effort to achieve
> affirmation and encouragement.

Let me block out a small parable that may help

> get my point
> across a bit better.

Benjamin Franklin did not invent lightning and electricity; he discovered and harnessed their power. There were all kinds of stories in folklore about where lightning came from. In the years to follow, men have built on the study of scientists before them to produce unbelievable uses for the phenomenon of electricity. Each new discovery adds to the body of knowledge. Men who follow are able to take what has been found and explore further.

So with the *person*. You will continually find out new things about your makeup; you will have broad experiences of all kinds that add to your perspective on life. The mature and wise person learns to stay aware of the new discoveries being made in his own life and to assimilate new experiences in the awareness that each new step makes life richer and broader.

By wearing various masks in *personage*

> the *person* grows
> like the body of knowledge
> about electricity
> has grown.

Perhaps this personal experience

> will help me
> make my point
> a bit more clearly.

I was having a great deal of struggle

> coming to believe
> that I had very much worth
> as a person.

I sought the able counsel of a friend.

> Our conversations
> proved to be
> a pivotal point
> in my life—

by that I mean
I have never been
the same
because of his help.

It was he who first pointed out to me

the mask-problem:
"All your life
you've worn a mask
of living up to expectations and pressures
trying to get approval and acceptance;
in the meantime
a real person has grown up
behind your mask
and you've never gotten acquainted
with yourself!"

I had value?

I had worth?

That was gospel to me—

and *gospel*
means
"good news!"

Starting then I began to peek behind the mask

and guess what—
I liked me!

It finally helped me to realize that Jesus was always

> looking behind other people's masks
> and saying to them:
> "God loves you
> *just* like
>   and sometimes
>   *even* like
>   you are!"

He spent his lifetime affirming people who were busy

> living Halloween
> instead of Easter!

I was amazed that he condemned only the ones

> who wanted to force
> people to be
> what some people thought
> they should be.

His greatest encouragement and words of love

> went to men like
> Zacchaeus
>   Nicodemus
>   Blind Bartimaeus
>   Matthew
>   Peter
>   Paul
> because they were willing

to try the life
of real people . . .

persons, if you please.

I am a person—

unmasked
open
searching
becoming
being
falling
rising
loving.

A mask is a crutch to support real personality;

lean on it while you must;
shun it when you can;
stand tall
you are a *person!*

Hi ho!

SAINT CHARLIE THE BROWN

You know him well, old Charlie Brown . . .

> zigzagged polo shirt
> > dog-food pan in hand
> > > kite up a tree
> > > > managing a losing team
> > > > shamed by Lucy.

Go on . . . you do it all the time . . .

> erase his name
> and write in yours.

You long to hear "I love you"

> > > "You are important to me"
> > > "You are special"
> > > "You have ability"
> > > "You have worth"
> and all you hear is
> > > "Good grief!"

With head hung low beneath the kite-eating tree

> you embrace your only friend, Snoopy,
> and you're not sure *he* really loves you
> because he can't talk.

Lonely as a ghost in a fog—or are you?

Self-awareness is like a dawn

> and not
> like
> a flashbulb.

Jesus heard the heavenly Father say

> "This is my beloved Son
> in whom I am pleased"
> at the *outset* of his ministry
> not at the *end* of it.

Go on, Charlie,

> unwrap your gift
> and find out what you're worth.

CHAPTER 3

OF WORTH

(Or, "The Gospel According to Cinderella")

There you stand—the princess of the kingdom
   in rags
   mopping the cellar
   for your
   lazy stepmother
   and ugly stepsisters.

Cinderella!

   The fantasy-heroine
   of every girl
   who ever tried
   Mother's high heels.

How lovely you are, you the hope
   of multitudes
   because both
     a godmother
     and
     a prince
   found you.

All your diamonds till then were in the rough—
> coal to be exact—
> and your life
> was dull
>> lonely
>> twisted
>> worthless.

Certainly you must smile a deep smile
> remembering the fear
> that struck your mopper's heart
> when tiny bells jangled
> lights swirled
> and the fairy godmother
> spoke your name.

Pre-ball hysteria, you must have thought—
> wanting to go
> so desperately
> but knowing
> you couldn't dare dream it.

A few minor miracles later
> on your way
> in your pumpkin-coach,
> mouse-drawn,
> to the castle.

In the arms of the handsome prince
        you swirled the night
        floating like soft down
        over the marble floor.

What conflict! Loving the prince
        hating the clock
        clutching his hand in fear
        running for the coach
        as the chimes buried your joy
        and you returned to reality
        in tears.

What a comedown!
        Home to rags
        after a ball like that.

Days later a buzz in the halls upstairs—
        the prince,
            slipper in hand,
        at the door
        searching the land
        for the beautiful lady
        who had won his heart.

Yours fluttered as he fruitlessly tried the slipper
        on the sisters—
        glad in your heart
        that its mini-size
        would not fit
        their maxi-feet!

"No one else here except the scrubgirl"
        said the evil stepmother,
        sisters seconding the motion.

"May I see her"
        said the prince.
        I like him—
           like his great faith in
             the unlikely!

Not blinded nor hindered by
        rags
          mop water
            sweat
               or bare feet
        he kneels
        to try the shoe
        on *your* foot!

Cinderella, is it joy
        confidence
        fear
        or all three
        as you look in his eyes
        and slip on your shoe?

The shoe on your foot

your hand to his lips
your soul on wings
your stepmother in a faint!

And now as princess at his side
you know the meaning of love
like so few.

You! Cinderella reading this page right now . . .
how's *your* cellar?
dark?
damp?
lonely?

Ever feel that the whole world is going to a ball
while you stay home
in rags
to mop the cellar?

Swish a few more suds on the red tile floor
while you ponder this one:
was Cinderella
a princess in rags
or a scrubgirl who became
a princess?

This is where the "gospel according to Cinderella"
gets to be good news—
she was a princess
in rags
with all the possibility

waiting to be
set free.

Our big word in this chapter is "worth"
meaning value
significance
importance.

You should see a strong relation
between this chapter
and the last one . . .
the scrubgirl was the *personage,*
the princess was the *person.*

This amplifies a basic principle in life:
most of us see ourselves
in the "scrubgirl" role—
wasting away
in dingy halls
dominated by others
afraid to exert ourselves
even with the help
of the believing godmother!

There is a whole kingdom awaiting the person
who learns his own worth
and finds his joy
in the midst of life.

It was so for numerous biblical characters
Abraham

Joseph
David
Peter (especially Peter!)
Paul
and Mary.

The main word for man in the Scriptures is love
and love is best understood
in another word:
grace.

Grace has a lot of official definitions.
I like to think of it
as God
with a glass slipper
in his hand.

Jesus said it:
"I came to seek
and to save . . ."

Like a string through beautiful pearls
the idea of
God as seeker
ties the Scriptures together.

I have an idea that you are like most people
accepting the idea
when it relates to
old people long ago
or unusual cases today

but
unwilling to believe
that your life can be changed
and that you can find
a sense of worth and value.

That's the heart of the Christian faith:

God sees a princess
in every scrubgirl
a free man
in every slave
a son
in every stranger.

Michelangelo was once asked:
"How do you manage
to create
these beautiful sculptures?"

Pointing to an angel he had just finished
he replied:
"I saw the angel
in the marble
and just chiseled
until I set him free!"

I'm sitting here as I write these words
listening to a record
of Jose Feliciano
playing guitar.

I get chords out of a guitar—
        he gets music!
        And *how* he gets music!

Something like that happens
        when God sees the angel in your marble
          strums the melody in your strings
          slips the slipper on your foot.

Furthermore, there are many "princes"
        at work in the world—
          teachers
          parents
          sweethearts
          friends
          ministers—
        who see angels in your marble.

That means there are many sources
        from which you may learn
        the meaning
        of your personal worth.

Our sentence so far reads:
        "I am
        a person
        of worth . . ."

The Scripture shouts it like the captain of a Navy ship:
        "Now
        hear
        this!"

Let me share a very personal story
        of how this
        principle of worth
        has affected
        my family.

My son, Toby, is a Charlie Brown fan
        of the first order.

On a trip together he was reading his favorite
        cartoon strips
        to the family;
        we were all laughing
        and having a great time
        together.

I changed the mood a bit
        by asking Toby
        to name his favorite
        character in *Peanuts,*
        at least the one
        he felt was most like
        himself.

He said, as most of us would, I think:
        "Charlie Brown."

I then asked him which of the characters
        reminded him most
        of his older brother, Perry.
        With a snappy look
        he remarked: "Lucy!"

I asked Perry the same questions:
               he also felt like
               Charlie Brown;
               to him, Toby was
               Linus!

We spent the next few miles
               talking about
               only the strong points
               about the three characters:
               Charlie Brown, Lucy, and Linus.

I then turned the conversation
               more directly to
               the boys themselves.

I asked them to name only the strong points
               about one another.
               This took time
               but it presented
               some beautiful insights.

My wife and I then entered in
               and shared our feelings
               about each of them;
               then we took our turn
               letting the family
               talk about the things
               they really liked
               in each of us.

I have never been as uncomfortable
        in all my life
        as I was
        listening to my family
        name my strengths
        and affirm my worth.

At the end of the brief experiment
        each of us
        fought to hide tears
        as we received
        the good gift of love
        and sensed our worth
        in one another's eyes.

The family has never been the same
        and I certainly have not.

Many people have knelt before me
        with slipper in hand
        to affirm my worth;
        none ever meant more
        than these most dear to me.

I am declares your uniqueness;
        a person acknowledges the dimension
        in your life
        growing behind the shaping forces;
        of worth points to your meaning
          in the eyes of God

as an object of his search
and a son in his kingdom.

Perhaps he just tapped your shoulder
in your cellar.
Cinderella . . .
go have a ball!

WHO PAINTED THAT ONE?

The one over there on the south wall

    with all the black
             red
              gray
                  orange . . .
    who painted it?

Oh, Robinson, eh? Sam . . .

    it's a Robinson!

You knew it? How?

    Hmmm . . . right, I see it—
    the slash of light right through the center . . .
    really? He does that in every picture?
    Sounds like some kind of trademark, then . . .

That must be one over there, too . . .

    yes . . . the green shanty
        with the prospector and mule
        out front . . .
                I could tell it
                by the slash of light
                right through the center.

You know, that is really cool . . .

    putting something like that
    in every painting . . .
                bet not many people
                know that about
                Robinson.

And so it was in the days of self-awareness

    that man came to see
    the slash of light
    through his center . . .
                put in every one
                by God himself.

                        That's image!

CHAPTER 4

CREATED IN THE IMAGE OF GOD

First, a question:

>   what is your favorite
>   verse of Scripture?

Most of us choose John 3:16

>   or some other
>   which we can
>   remember.

I have had a change of heart in this area

>   within the past
>   three years.

This verse is not only my favorite,

>   it

changed
my
life.

John 1:14 it is . . .

"The word became flesh
and walked
among us."

It was a rowdy sort of character

in a college dorm
bull session
that made me think
this verse over
for the first time
in years.

We were talking about Jesus as a human being

and I was noting
that most of us
don't really believe
that he was as much *man*
as he was *God*.

I was attempting to prove my point

in some fantastic fashion
by showing that

most of us think
he never hit his thumb in the carpenter shop
   never wore Band-Aids with new sandals
   never thought Jewish girls were pretty
   never got annoyed
      walking out
      slamming the tent flap!

To further force the group to wrestle with the problem

I posed a hypothetical,
imaginary situation.

Jesus is walking from Jerusalem to Bethany

to visit Mary, Martha, and Lazarus.
It is 2:00 A.M.
there are no street lights
he is alone.

Out there by himself as he is

he stumps his toe
on a big rock,
splits the nail back
on the great toe
and is now hopping around
on his good foot
holding his hurt foot.

My question to the students in the dorm was:

Now, what do you think
he said
at that point?

Like lightning striking, the answer came

from our rowdy friend
in the back of the group:

"Hosanah?"

We all broke up!

You may chuckle at that

but it is a truth:
We want him to say "Hosanah"
when he stumps his toe!

At that precise moment John1:14 flashed in my mind

with new meaning
for all time
and it hung around
to haunt me
for the months
since.

My point is this:

you and I

have not genuinely considered
his humanity
and his development
as a person.

He did grow in wisdom and stature

and in favor
with man
and God.

Consider now a crucial point in his life:

he did not begin
his earthly ministry
until he
was
thirty
years
of age!

And how he began is the point of our chapter:

it talks about being created
in the image of God.

Put your thinking cap on for a few minutes

and pursue the meaning
of the phrase:
image of God.

Time out.

Time in.

Ready? We were at the point of the beginning

of his
earthly ministry.

How did he begin?

He came to John the Baptist
to be baptized
then he went away
into the wilderness
to face the options
open to him in his ministry.

Satan is reported to have tried several offers

each of which
was promptly
refused by our Lord.

This episode in his life is generally tagged

"The Temptations of Jesus."

I got help here from a teacher.

He observed that these were not temptations

> as much as they were
> *decisions in the wilderness*,

This remarkable young man

> with all his gifts
> and with his unique
> relation to God—
> he even called God
> the word we would translate
> *Daddy*—
> still had to decide
>   who would rule his life
>   what he would do with his life.

His entire life after this wilderness venture

> is lived against
> the backdrop
> of those decisions.

In my opinion this is the crux

> of the idea
> of
> *the image of God*.

The concept contains many facets

        like the cuts
        on a beautiful diamond.

However, supremely in our consideration

        is the fact
        that God has given each of us—
        are you paying close attention now?—
        the capacity to make decisions
            to make commitments
            to say *yes* and *no*
            to direct our lives!

That is what makes you different from

        a fossil
        a fig
          a fox
            a fish.

You have the right to determine

        your values
          goals
          companions
          vocation
          character.

You have the same option with your parents

>   to love them
>   to hate them.

You are a person of worth

>   (imagine herald trumpets
>   and rolling drums)
>   *created in the image of God.*

Free!

>   to decide
>   choose
>   love
>   help
>   hurt
>   covet
>   abuse
>   support
>   enrich.

It then becomes crucial

>   how we make decisions
>   and direct our lives.

I can point to none other than Jesus Christ

>   as the model

and example
for clear-cut decisions
and keen
life-directing.

His principle was this:

I am God's Son.
God is love.
God is self-giving.
I will take God's love seriously.
I will live my life
        so that men
        shall know God
        more clearly
        because I passed this way.

And he did.
And it killed him.

Difficult decisions that put God's love to work

in our world
are not easy—
then or now.

Like the commercial, he calls you

to come all the way up
to God's kind
of living.

Like the warning on the package

        it may be harmful
        to your health.

The most unbelievable fact about being created

        in his image
        is that you are free
        to reject him.

My concern is that although you may be

        that free
        that you will not be
        that foolish.

Two chapters back I recommended my friend, Dan Webster.

        Now I want to recommend
        my best friend . . .
                    Jesus Christ.

Being created in the image of God

        also gives you the freedom
        to become increasingly
        like him.

See yourself like a pilgrim at Plymouth

with a vast world before you
that needs the best you can give
and will take the best you offer
and then give it your best.

It's a big decision . . .

go on, Cinderella . . .

put your foot
in
the
slipper!

ALONE IS MORE THAN A WORD

Solitaire wouldn't be such a bad game

     if you didn't have
     to play it
     by yourself.

One is, indeed, the loneliest word

     in the dictionary.

I'm glad, God, that you thought of

     groups
      teams
       families
        communities
         couples
          partners
      hand-holding
       hugging
        patting-on-the-head
         snuggling
      togetherness
      nearness.

What tragedy to accomplish a fantastic feat

     on a desert island
     and try to impress
     a gull and a bug
     with your prowess . . .

What joy to burst in on a friend and say

     "Look what I did!"
     "Look who I am!"
     "Look at me!"
         or a thousand other
         things
         that were not meant
         to be borne   alone!

Even God
    is
   a
    trinity . . .

CHAPTER 5

TO RELATE

So far in this book we have been considering

the developing person
created by God
with personal worth
and freedom of choice . . .

now we come
to put that egg
in the basket
with all the other eggs.

You were not created a hermit

or a lonesome pine;
you were created
as a person
and that means
    you need other persons

like a fish needs water
a bird needs feathers
a child needs parents
a flower needs spring!

The book of Genesis has a great way of putting it:

Adam is created
to caretake the garden
name the animals
enjoy creation.

The giraffe had other giraffes

the whale had other whales
the aardvark had other aardvarks
the louse had other lice.

God is pictured as saying:

"Lice have it better than Adam"
or, more scripturally,
"It is not good that man should be alone."

Enter Eve.

Helpmate.
  Curious.
    Woman.

The act of creation teaches many things

about where we came from
about where the created order came from

but

I see a lesson
that is the foundation
for this chapter:

Adam could not
understand Adam
relating only to
giraffes
aardvarks
whales
and lice.

A very wise man I had never heard of

wrote something
I never read before

which I read recently
in the December, 1970,
National Geographic:

"Though I am different
from you
We were born involved
in one another."
(T'ao Ch'ien A.D. 365–427)

That means you cannot understand you

without other persons
in your garden.

Most of us have other persons there.

The problem is
relating to them.

For the insights I now share with you

a tip of the hat
to Dr. Thomas A. Harris,
author of
I'm O.K., You're O.K.

He maintains that there are four basic life positions:

I'm not o.k., you're o.k.
I'm not o.k., you're not o.k.

I'm o.k., you're not o.k.
I'm o.k., you're o.k.

That's more o.k.'s than you generally see

> if you inspect
> television sets
> for Sylvania!

Let's look at these positions

> to see
> what we can learn
> about ourselves.

First, *I'm not o.k., You're o.k.*
This is the basic self-other understanding

> we see in ourselves
> as we begin our lives
> as children
> in families.

Parents stand as examples

> of all the things we must learn
> > acts we must perform
> > > persons we must imitate
> in order to be
> acceptable in life.

Dr. Harris believes that every child

> regardless of family situation
> comes into the world
> with the basic concept
> that he is *not o.k.*

The other word for "not o.k." is one

> with which
> you are familiar:
> > *inferiority.*

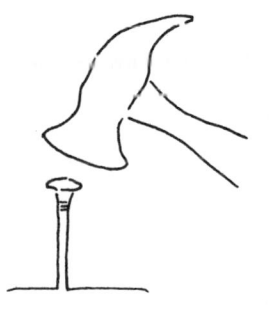

He hits the nail on the head

> when he points out
> the fact
> that man lives his life
> attempting to overcome
> his feelings of
> inferiority.

Some come to feel that no matter what they do

> they are still
> not o.k.

Others, fortunately, come to experience

> affirming and supportive
> situations in life
> that can help them see
> that they are
> really o.k. persons.

Summary on position 1:

> The basic life position is
> "I'm not o.k., you're o.k."
> and is the chief hurdle
> to clear.

Second, *I'm not o.k., You're not o.k.*

This life position is a reaction to

> or modification of
> the first position.

In this stance a person loses the essential support

> from adults
> in the form of
> "stroking". . .
> > physical and emotional
> > affirmations that run
> > all the way from pats
> > on the head to saying

"I love you" and
"You matter to me."

A child generally begins to feel this vacuum

about the time
he begins walking
and he is not carried
and touched as much
as before.

The child concludes that he is *not o.k.*

because he cannot perform
all the necessary acts
that he is being groomed for . . .

bathroom,
self-feeding,
etc.

He then transfers his *not o.k.*-feelings

to the adults around him . . .
they are not o.k. because
they do not give back to him
the necessary feelings
that tell him he is o.k.

The terrible conclusion is

nobody is o.k. at all
and the world is bad . . .

> I suspect
> a great many suicides
> result
> from this feeling.

Summary on position 2:

> Loss of supportive
> and affirming love
> from parents and other key persons
> causes an individual
> to feel that what he has concluded
> about himself—"I'm not o.k."—
> applies to everyone . . .
>> hopelessness
>> faithlessness
>> despair
>> result.

Third: *I'm o.k., You're not o.k.*

There are some individuals

> who are not just deprived
> of affirming and supportive
> "stroking"
> by parents and key persons;
>> they are abused
>>> physically and mentally
>>> and depersonalized
>>> by constant negative bombardment.

In life position two

> we noted the individual
> who was left out of
> the stroking and affirming;
> in this position we see a person
> experiencing a vast encounter
> with very bad relationships.

His conclusion is:

> I'm o.k.
>> (misunderstood
>> and
>> mistreated)
> but you're *not* o.k.
>> (for misunderstanding
>> and
>> mistreating me).

This kind of person goes through life

> refusing to look inward
>> never accepts responsibility for his mistakes
>>> always blames "them"
>>>> it's always "their fault."

This is the personality of the psychopathic criminal

> who feels
> "it's them or me"

and grabs all he can
wherever he can.

Summary on position 3:

No affirming and supportive stroking
plus abusive treatment
from family and key persons
creates only suspicion
hatred
selfishness
bitterness.

Self is never at fault.
The world is out to get him.

Fourth: *I'm o.k., You're o.k.*

This is the position of hope

which best exemplifies
wisdom
self-appreciation
maturity.

The first three positions are mainly unconscious

> coming to us in early childhood
> when we have no experiences
> by which to evaluate life.

The fourth position is the conscious, intentional one

> and it is based on
> > thought
> > faith
> > > commitment
> > > decision.

The first three positions are based on feelings

> about experiences we have had
> which we have no way
> to evaluate
> at an early age.

Here we are talking about the person
> who comes to see
> that he has worth and meaning . . .
> he sees this in others, also.

Summary on position 4:

> *I'm o.k., You're o.k.*
> acknowledges both
> > the worth in self and
> > the worth in neighbor;

it further enables a person
to trust what he knows of himself
to what he knows of another.

So, we take another step in the basic sentence:

I am
  a person
    of worth
      created in the image of God
        to relate . . .

May I suggest another helpful insight on *relating?*

Learn to develop patience
as you struggle with another person
in developing a lasting relationship
knowing
    deep relationships
    don't just happen!

Another way, please . . .

mushrooms grow to maturity overnight
orchids take seven to twelve years to bloom.

Your relationships can be mushrooms or orchids . . .

the mature person
waits for orchids

but is patient
with mushrooms!

I have tried to say that you are basically afraid to risk yourself in a frenzied and frantic world, unsure of your best qualities, skeptical of others. Begin to see that you are *really* a person of worth and can relate to the best in others. In short, Self— *you're o.k.!*

MEDITATION ON A BEAUTIFUL KEY

There it is—right before your very eyes—
        my *key!*

What do you think of that

      all shiny
      brassy
      ridged
      smooth.

Some key, right?

      Probably you never saw
      a finer key in all your . . .
                 what?
                 What lock does
                 it fit?
      I have no idea.

But it is some more kind of key, right?

      Used to be my grandfather's
      and then my father's
      and now it's mine
            to guard
            keep
            protect
            pass on . . .

How should I know what lock it fits . . .

      would you
      please
      get off my back?

Some people have all the nerve . . .

      questions, questions, questions.

Who cares about locks

      when you have such
      a beauty of a key . . .

'Scuse me . . .

      I must go polish my key.

CHAPTER 6

TO LIVE

I have often wished I could talk to an old man

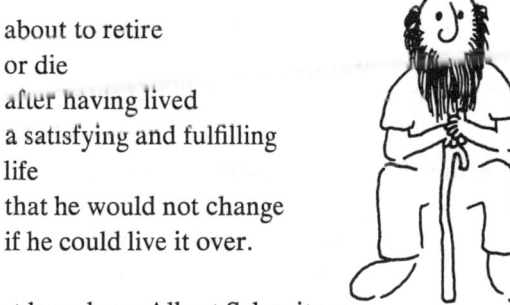

     about to retire
     or die
     after having lived
     a satisfying and fulfilling
     life
     that he would not change
     if he could live it over.

Such a man must have been Albert Schweitzer,

     missionary
     musician
     physician.

His entire life was lived out in the knowledge

     that he was doing

what he should be doing
where he should be doing it.

Interviews by numerous persons bear out the fact

that he would live his life
all over again
just the same way.

To me, this is the essence of living:

to look back
from the brink of death
with a solid smile
and say:
"I'm glad I did that!"

Through the history of man there have been

people with varied talents:
    carpenters
    painters
    musicians
    mothers
    athletes.

Their lives have been evidence of the spark of genius

so abundant
in life.

Imagine, if you can, life without

                 Brahms
                 Beethoven
                 Picasso
                     Winston Churchill
                     Johnny Unitas
                     Lew Alcindor
                         Glen Campbell.

Because of their exceptional gifts

                 life has been made different
                 for many men.

I honestly believe that there beats

                 in the breast
                 of every person
                 a desire
                 to exert a dramatic influence
                 on the course of life.

So far in this book we have been looking at *self*

                 with all
                 its possibilities
                 and potentials.

Allow the first five chapters to become a funnel

in your mind—
the wide, open end
that narrows down
to a slender neck—
and see this chapter as
the slender neck.

In the wide-mouth end of the book

we have talked about
your *I am*
with all its confusion
affirmation
joy
frustration;
your *person*
the real you
behind the masks
we all wear;
your *worth*
you, the princess in rags,
God before you
with the glass slipper in his hand;
your *power to decide*
image of God
ability to commit yourself
self-direction
freedom;
your *relationships*
learning to move from
I'm not o.k.

to
I'm o.k.

I am

> a person
> of worth
> created in the image of God
> to relate
> and
> to
> live!

So, now its up to

> Albert Schweitzer
> Glen Campbell
> and *you.*

I seem to do better getting my point over

> with the Cinderella-type
> material;
> try me with
> Simon Peter.

I have for some time seen Simon

> as the
> stumbling
> bumbling
> fumbling

> Barney Fife,
> deputy of Mayberry, USA.

His relationship with Jesus Christ

> reminds me
> of Barney's relationship
> with Andy Griffith:
>> of all the people
>> in town
>> only Andy
>> really saw the worth
>> in Barney
>> (prince-Cinderella reminder).

Nowhere is this more dramatically shown for me

> than on the night
> of the arrest of Jesus
> by the Temple guard.

We have always heard that Peter was a coward

> denying
> that he ever knew
> Jesus.

Let's take a closer look

> and see
> if that be

an accurate picture . . .

Jesus said in the upper room

> on that ill-fated night
> that one of the disciples
> would betray him.

Barney—excuse me, I slipped—*Peter,*

> in that
> Don Knotts-know-it-all
> attitude, says:
> > "Well, Lord, you're looking at one man
> > you can count on! Never catch me doing
> > something like that. In fact, I'd lay
> > down my life before I'd betray you!"

You are familiar with the story through here . . .

> to the garden to pray
> sleeping disciples
> > "Could not you watch one hour?"
> > the coming of the soldiers
> > > Peter grabs a sword, lops off an ear
> > > Jesus reprimands him
> > > the arrest is made
> > > > Jesus is taken away for trial.

The Scriptures tell us that at this point

      the disciples
      scattered for safety
      like a covey of quail.

Jesus is taken to the home of the high priest

      and Simon comes
      to the courtyard
      of the home
      where he is confronted
      three times
      by persons who claim
      to recognize him as
      a disciple of Jesus.

He has been branded a coward and traitor

      through the centuries
      for his statements
      that he did not know Jesus.

Note an interesting fact, will you?

      The first encounter is at the gate;
        the second in the center of the courtyard;
          the third at the very porch!

His denials are evidently an effort to conceal

his identity
as he works in closer
> either to attempt a rescue of Jesus
> or
> to size the situation up
>> before returning to the others.

With the possible exception of John

> Peter is the only disciple
> who did not flee!

The horror of the evening came after the third denial—

> immediately after saying
> "I never knew him!"
> accompanied by fisherman talk
> he heard footsteps behind him
> and turned to see Jesus being led away . . .
> He had heard! and Simon couldn't explain
> without breaking his disguise!

Simon went out and wept bitterly;

> the crucifixion was especially painful
> because he had not explained to Jesus

what he was doing
when he claimed not to be a disciple.

But remember the resurrection morning, Easter I—

Jesus tells the women
to go tell the disciples
that he is risen . . .
and Simon!

That was the gospel of acceptance and understanding

Andy Griffith-Barney Fife style;
Jesus, like Andy, said
"I understand, bungler!"

That was when Simon started to live

with reckless courage
zest
meaning
understanding.

Genuine, untarnished, long-lasting living

begins and is sustained
when we know without doubt
that we can try, fail, try, fail, try, fail . . .
and that God
accepts and understands us.

That is where it hits you, *Cinderella Fife*—

> real living
> is fellowship with God . . .
>> and, thanks be!
>> He is like Jesus
>> and not like an imperfect human.

Jesus did not come to leave a list of rules;

> he came to tell us
> that God is like
>> the father waiting for the prodigal
>> the shepherd looking for his sheep
>> the watcher after lilies, sparrows, and hairs.

A friend once told me of a quirk of his that is funny to me:

> he cannot throw away
> a key . . .
>> skeleton
>>> Yale
>>>> suitcase
>>>>> or door.

He has a shoebox full of keys

> which disturbed his wife
> on one occasion
> when they were moving.

She wanted to discard them . . .

> he nearly
> had soul failure!

She asked him outright, finally,

> if he could tell her
> what lock any one key
> in the box might fit;
> he could not name one
> lock/key combination.

We laughed as he told me that, and then it hit me:

> so much of our life
> in the church
> has been spent
> guarding a box of keys
> to locks that no longer exist
>> that have no current meaning
>> that cannot be remembered.

Don't let anyone tell you that real living

is guarding a box of old keys
that do not fit any current locks.

Real living is to be found within

what the Bible calls
eternal life.

You usually hear that used to describe

unending
perpetual
forever-and-forever
everlasting life.

However, the idea of eternal life

does not carry
with it
the idea of *length*
as much as it does
the idea of *depth.*

It has to do with a quality of life

that strives toward
the quality demonstrated
by Jesus Christ . . .
full of turning the other cheek
walking the second mile
loving his enemies
returning good for evil
seeing the best in others.

This brings up again my key Scripture verse:

"The word of God
became a human being
and walked among us."

You are a person created in the image of God
to relate and
to live
like he lived!

BIBLIOGRAPHY

Harris, Thomas A. *I'm O.K., You're O.K.* New York: Harper and Row, 1967.

Havighurst, Robert J. *Human Development and Education.* New York: David McKay Company, Inc., 1953.

Oates, Wayne E. *The Religious Dimensions of Personality.* New York: Association Press, 1957.

Southard, Samuel. *The Imperfect Disciple.* Nashville: Broadman Press, 1968.

Tournier, Paul. *The Meaning of Persons.* New York: Harper and Row, 1957.

ACKNOWLEDGEMENTS

The art work throughout the text of the book is the work of Sharon Baugh from Dallas, Texas. We have had many long talks about the theme of the book. Her work has really been the "icing on the cake."

I wish to thank in particular two of my most revered and honored friends, Wayne E. Oates and Samuel Southard. From 1960–1964 I attended the Southern Baptist Theological Seminary, graduating in 1964 with the Bachelor of Divinity degree. The two most dramatic and life-changing courses in my college and graduate divinity education were taught by these two men. I have relied heavily on class notes from Psychology 151 with Southard and Psychology 156 with Oates for insights and ideas in this book.

They have both been more than teachers and friends.
They have been light in darkness
                    hope in confusion
                    strength in weakness
                    and above all . . .

                                        they bugged
                                        my self!